INNOVATIONS IN RESPIRATORY MEDICINE

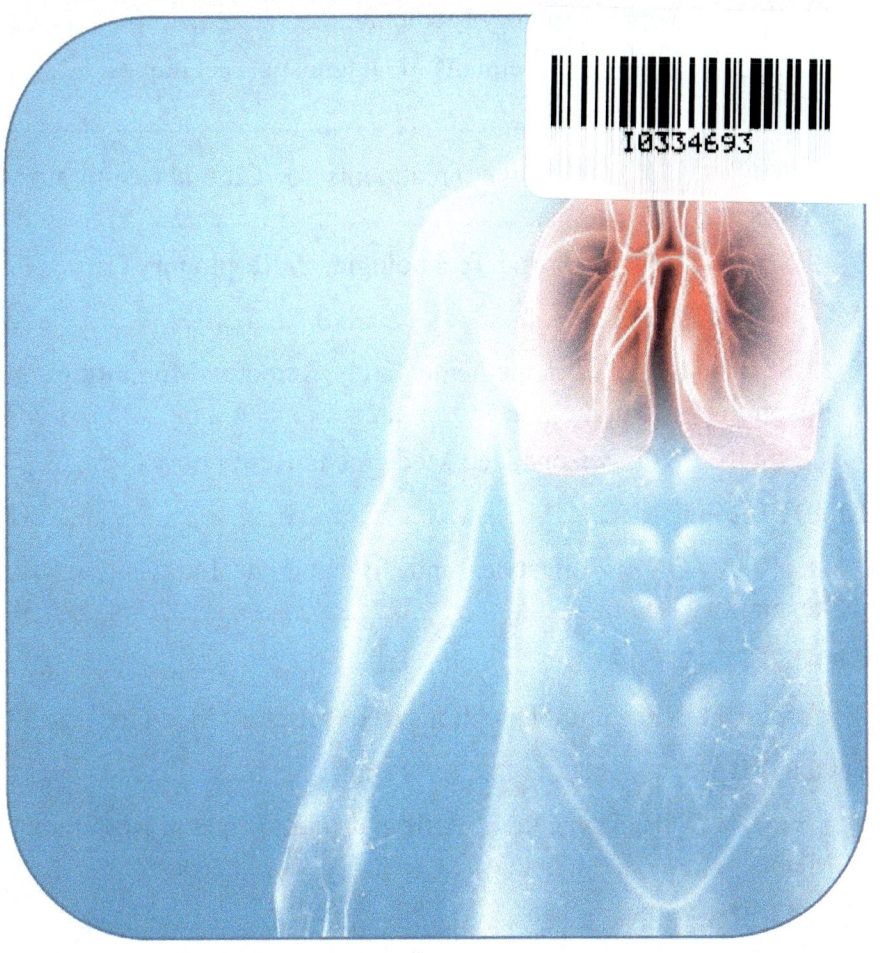

TABLE OF CONTENTS

INTRODUCTION 2
MODULE ONE 3
   LESSON ONE: Respiratory Medicine 3
   LESSON TWO: Advancements in Diagnostic Techniques 7
MODULE TWO 12
   LESSON ONE: Innovative Treatments for Chronic Respiratory Diseases 12
   LESSON TWO: Emerging Technologies in Respiratory Care 17
MODULE THREE 22
   LESSON ONE: Telemedicine and Remote Monitoring in Respiratory Medicine 22
   LESSON TWO: Personalized Medicine in Respiratory Care 27
MODULE FOUR 32
   LESSON ONE: Lifestyle and Behavioral Interventions in Respiratory Health 32
MODULE FIVE 37
   LESSON ONE: Future Directions in Respiratory Medicine 37
MODULE SIX 41
   LESSON ONE: The Role of Artificial Intelligence in Respiratory Medicine 41
MODULE SEVEN 46
   LESSON ONE: The Importance of Interdisciplinary Collaboration in Respiratory Medicine 46
CONCLUSION 51
REFERENCES 52

COURSE OVERVIEW

This course on provides a comprehensive exploration of the latest advancements, technologies, and interdisciplinary approaches shaping the field of respiratory medicine. Through a series of interactive lectures, case studies, and discussions, participants will gain a deep understanding of the innovative strategies, diagnostic tools, therapeutic interventions, and collaborative practices driving progress in respiratory care.

COURSE OBJECTIVES

The objectives of this course is to let participant learn about emerging diagnostic tools, imaging techniques, and biomarker assays that enable early detection, accurate diagnosis, and personalized treatment planning for a wide range of respiratory conditions. The course will cover innovative therapeutic strategies, including targeted therapies, immunomodulatory agents, and gene-based treatments, as well as the role of precision medicine in optimizing treatment outcomes for patients with respiratory diseases and allow participants will explore the integration of technology-driven solutions, such as virtual reality, wearable devices, and telemedicine platforms, in respiratory rehabilitation programs and patient management, enhancing engagement, adherence, and outcomes.

COURSE MATERIALS

To learn this course, **healthcare providers/ participants** must be provided with materials like a Pen, pencil, notebook, and notepad to better understand and make it easy for them to learn.

INTRODUCTION

Welcome to "Innovations in Respiratory Medicine: A Comprehensive Course for Healthcare Providers." This book aims to serve as a definitive guide for healthcare professionals seeking to expand their knowledge and expertise in the rapidly evolving field of respiratory medicine. Respiratory health is a cornerstone of overall well-being, and advancements in this field have the potential to significantly enhance patient outcomes and quality of life. As medical science progresses, staying abreast of the latest innovations becomes not just beneficial but essential for practitioners dedicated to providing the highest standard of care.

This comprehensive course is structured to provide a deep dive into the latest advancements, technologies, and methodologies that are revolutionizing respiratory medicine. Each lesson is meticulously crafted to cover various aspects of respiratory care, from cutting-edge diagnostic tools to innovative treatment modalities and emerging trends that promise to shape the future of this critical field. By the end of this book, you will have gained a holistic understanding of the contemporary landscape of respiratory medicine and be well-equipped to implement these innovations in your practice.

MODULE ONE

LESSON ONE: RESPIRATORY MEDICINE

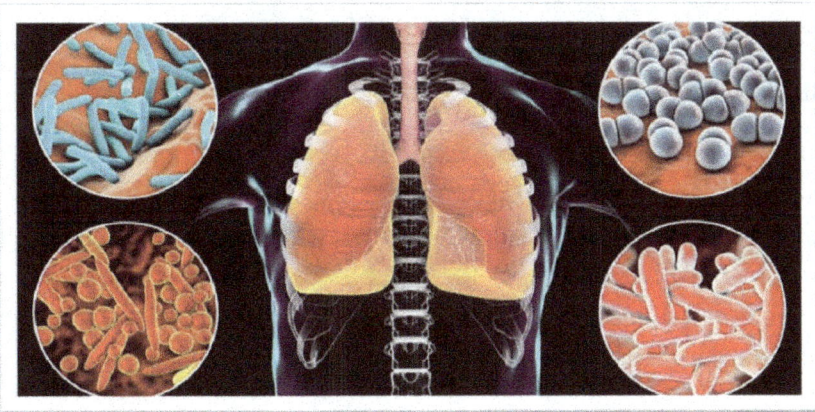

Respiratory medicine, also known as pulmonology, is a vital branch of medicine focused on the diagnosis, treatment, and prevention of diseases affecting the respiratory system. The respiratory system, comprising the lungs, airways, and respiratory muscles, is essential for gas exchange, supplying oxygen to the body, and removing carbon dioxide. Disorders of this system can significantly impact overall health and quality of life, making the study and advancement of respiratory medicine critically important.

Historical Perspective

The history of respiratory medicine is rich with significant milestones that have shaped the field. Early descriptions of respiratory diseases can be traced back to ancient civilizations. For instance, the ancient Egyptians and Greeks documented conditions resembling asthma and tuberculosis. Hippocrates, often referred to as the father of medicine, wrote extensively about respiratory symptoms and their possible causes.

The understanding of respiratory diseases progressed significantly during the Renaissance with the advent of anatomical studies.

Andreas Vesalius, a pioneering anatomist, made detailed observations of the respiratory system, which laid the groundwork for future discoveries. The invention of the microscope in the 17th century by Antonie van Leeuwenhoek further propelled the field, allowing scientists to observe microorganisms, including those responsible for respiratory infections.

Fundamentals of Respiratory Physiology

Understanding the basic physiology of the respiratory system is crucial for appreciating the complexities of respiratory medicine. The primary function of the respiratory system is to facilitate gas exchange, which occurs in the alveoli of the lungs. Oxygen from inhaled air diffuses into the bloodstream, while carbon dioxide from the blood diffuses into the alveoli to be exhaled.

The mechanics of breathing involve the coordinated efforts of the respiratory muscles, including the diaphragm and intercostal muscles. The diaphragm's contraction creates negative pressure in the thoracic cavity, allowing air to flow into the lungs. Relaxation of the diaphragm and elastic recoil of the lungs facilitate exhalation.

Common Respiratory Diseases

A wide range of diseases can affect the respiratory system, ranging from acute infections to chronic conditions. Some of the most prevalent respiratory diseases include:

- Asthma: A chronic inflammatory disease characterized by airway hyperresponsiveness and reversible airflow obstruction. Symptoms include wheezing, shortness of breath, and coughing.
- Chronic Obstructive Pulmonary Disease (COPD): A group of progressive lung diseases, including chronic bronchitis and emphysema, that cause obstructed airflow and breathing difficulties. Smoking is a major risk factor.

- Pneumonia: An infection that inflames the air sacs in one or both lungs, which may fill with fluid or pus. It can be caused by bacteria, viruses, or fungi.
- Tuberculosis (TB): A bacterial infection caused by Mycobacterium tuberculosis that primarily affects the lungs but can spread to other organs.
- Pulmonary Fibrosis: A condition characterized by scarring of the lung tissue, leading to progressive and irreversible decline in lung function.

Diagnostic Approaches in Respiratory Medicine

Accurate diagnosis is the cornerstone of effective respiratory care. Various diagnostic tools and techniques are employed to assess the function and structure of the respiratory system:

- Pulmonary Function Tests (PFTs): These tests measure lung volumes, capacities, and flow rates to diagnose and monitor respiratory conditions. Spirometry is a common PFT that measures the amount and speed of air a person can inhale and exhale.
- Imaging Techniques: Chest X-rays, computed tomography (CT) scans, and magnetic resonance imaging (MRI) provide detailed images of the lungs and airways, aiding in the diagnosis of diseases such as pneumonia, lung cancer, and interstitial lung disease.
- Bronchoscopy: A procedure that allows direct visualization of the airways using a flexible tube with a camera. It can be used for diagnostic purposes, such as taking biopsies, or therapeutic interventions, like removing obstructions.
- Blood Gas Analysis: This test measures the levels of oxygen and carbon dioxide in the blood, providing insights into the respiratory system's efficiency in gas exchange.

Advancements in Respiratory Medicine

The field of respiratory medicine has witnessed remarkable advancements over the years, driven by research and technological innovations. These advancements have significantly improved diagnostic accuracy, treatment efficacy, and patient outcomes. Some notable innovations include:

- Biologic Therapies: The development of biologic drugs targeting specific pathways involved in diseases like asthma and COPD has revolutionized treatment options. These therapies offer more personalized and effective management of chronic respiratory conditions.
- Minimally Invasive Techniques: Advances in bronchoscopy and thoracic surgery have led to less invasive procedures, reducing recovery times and improving patient outcomes. Techniques like endobronchial ultrasound (EBUS) and video-assisted thoracoscopic surgery (VATS) are examples of such innovations.
- Telemedicine: The integration of telemedicine in respiratory care has expanded access to specialist consultations and continuous monitoring, particularly in remote and underserved areas. This has been especially crucial during the COVID-19 pandemic, enabling remote management of chronic respiratory diseases and reducing the risk of exposure.

DISCUSSION QUESTIONS

- What are the key drivers behind the advancements in respiratory medicine, and how have these innovations transformed the field in recent years?
- What are some of the major challenges and unmet needs in respiratory medicine that innovations aim to address, and how can healthcare providers and researchers collaborate to overcome these challenges?

LESSON TWO: ADVANCEMENTS IN DIAGNOSTIC TECHNIQUES

In the realm of respiratory medicine, accurate diagnosis is paramount to the effective management and treatment

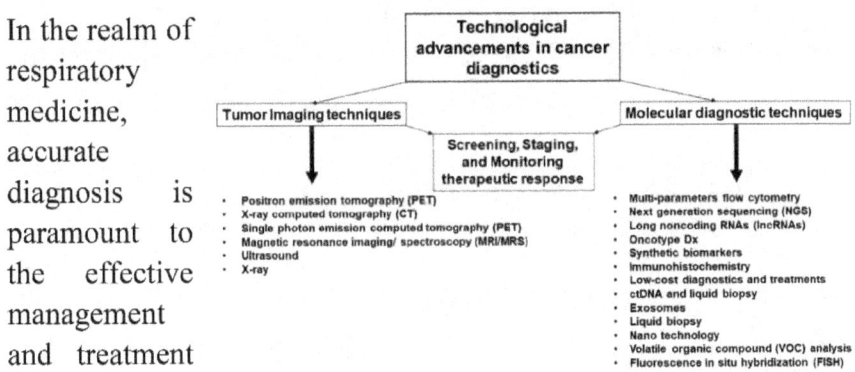

of respiratory diseases. The advent of advanced diagnostic techniques has revolutionized the field, enabling earlier detection, precise characterization, and comprehensive monitoring of respiratory conditions. This lesson delves into the cutting-edge diagnostic tools and methodologies that are reshaping respiratory care, highlighting their principles, applications, and impacts on patient outcomes.

High-Resolution Imaging Techniques

Imaging plays a crucial role in the diagnosis and monitoring of respiratory diseases. Advances in imaging technology have significantly enhanced the resolution and clarity of images, allowing for more detailed visualization of the lungs and airways.

- High-Resolution Computed Tomography (HRCT): HRCT has become a cornerstone in the diagnosis of interstitial lung diseases and other diffuse parenchymal lung disorders. It provides detailed cross-sectional images of the lungs, revealing fine details of the lung parenchyma and aiding in the assessment of disease extent and pattern.
- Positron Emission Tomography (PET) Scans: PET scans, often combined with CT (PET/CT), are invaluable in the diagnosis and staging of lung cancer. They provide metabolic information about lung lesions, helping to differentiate

between benign and malignant nodules and assess the extent of cancer spread.
- Magnetic Resonance Imaging (MRI): Although less commonly used in pulmonary medicine compared to CT, MRI offers superior soft tissue contrast and can be useful in specific scenarios, such as evaluating vascular structures and mediastinal masses without ionizing radiation.

Advanced Pulmonary Function Tests (PFTs)

Pulmonary function tests are essential for assessing lung function and diagnosing respiratory disorders. Recent advancements have expanded the capabilities of these tests, providing more comprehensive insights into respiratory physiology.

- Impulse Oscillometry (IOS): IOS is a non-invasive technique that measures respiratory impedance, offering detailed information about airway resistance and reactance. It is particularly useful in patients who have difficulty performing traditional spirometry, such as young children and the elderly.
- Multiple Breath Washout (MBW): MBW tests evaluate ventilation distribution within the lungs and are particularly valuable in diagnosing and monitoring early-stage lung diseases, such as cystic fibrosis. This technique measures the efficiency of gas mixing in the lungs, providing insights into small airway function.
- Diffusing Capacity of the Lung for Carbon Monoxide (DLCO): DLCO tests measure the ability of the lungs to transfer gas from inhaled air to the bloodstream. This test is critical for diagnosing and monitoring diseases that affect the alveolar-capillary membrane, such as pulmonary fibrosis and emphysema.

Molecular and Genetic Testing

The integration of molecular and genetic testing into respiratory diagnostics has opened new avenues for personalized medicine, enabling targeted therapies based on individual genetic profiles.

- Genomic Sequencing: Next-generation sequencing (NGS) technologies allow for comprehensive genomic analysis, identifying mutations and genetic variations associated with respiratory diseases. This is particularly relevant in the management of lung cancer, where specific genetic mutations can guide the selection of targeted therapies.
- Biomarker Analysis: The identification of biomarkers in blood, sputum, or other biological samples provides valuable information about disease presence, severity, and progression. Biomarkers such as eosinophils and periostin are used in the management of asthma to guide the use of biologic therapies.
- Liquid Biopsy: Liquid biopsy involves the analysis of circulating tumor DNA (ctDNA) in blood samples, offering a non-invasive method for detecting and monitoring lung cancer. This technique enables the identification of genetic mutations and the assessment of treatment response without the need for invasive tissue biopsies.

Artificial Intelligence and Machine Learning

The application of artificial intelligence (AI) and machine learning (ML) in respiratory diagnostics is rapidly gaining traction, offering potential for improved accuracy, efficiency, and predictive capabilities.

- AI-Enhanced Imaging: AI algorithms are being developed to analyze imaging data, such as chest X-rays and CT scans, to detect abnormalities with high accuracy. These systems can assist radiologists by highlighting areas of concern and providing diagnostic suggestions, ultimately improving diagnostic efficiency and reducing human error.
- Predictive Analytics: ML models can analyze vast amounts of clinical data to predict disease outcomes and progression. For example, predictive analytics can identify patients at high risk of developing severe respiratory complications, enabling early intervention and personalized care plans.

- Automated Spirometry Interpretation: AI-based systems can automate the interpretation of spirometry results, identifying patterns indicative of specific respiratory diseases. This can streamline the diagnostic process and ensure consistent and accurate assessments.

Innovations in Bronchoscopy

Bronchoscopy, a procedure that allows direct visualization of the airways, has seen significant advancements, enhancing its diagnostic and therapeutic capabilities.

- Endobronchial Ultrasound (EBUS): EBUS combines bronchoscopy with ultrasound imaging, allowing for real-time visualization of structures surrounding the airways. This technique is invaluable for diagnosing and staging lung cancer, as it enables guided biopsies of lymph nodes and other mediastinal structures.
- Electromagnetic Navigation Bronchoscopy (ENB): ENB uses electromagnetic technology to create a virtual map of the airways, guiding the bronchoscope to peripheral lung lesions that are difficult to reach with traditional bronchoscopy. This technique improves the accuracy of biopsies and facilitates the diagnosis of early-stage lung cancer.
- Optical Coherence Tomography (OCT): OCT provides high-resolution cross-sectional images of the airways, similar to a "microscopic" view. This technique is used to assess airway wall structure and detect early changes associated with diseases like asthma and COPD.

The advancements in diagnostic techniques have profoundly transformed respiratory medicine, enabling earlier and more accurate diagnosis, personalized treatment planning, and better patient outcomes. High-resolution imaging, advanced pulmonary function tests, molecular and genetic testing, AI and ML applications, and innovative bronchoscopy techniques are just a few of the tools at the forefront of this revolution. As these technologies continue to evolve, they promise to further enhance our understanding and management of respiratory diseases, ultimately improving the quality of care provided to patients.

DISCUSSION QUESTIONS

- How have diagnostic technologies evolved in respiratory medicine, and what are some of the most promising advancements in diagnostic tools for respiratory diseases?
- What role do artificial intelligence and machine learning play in enhancing diagnostic capabilities in respiratory medicine, and what are the potential benefits and challenges associated with their integration into clinical practice?

MODULE TWO

LESSON ONE: INNOVATIVE TREATMENTS FOR CHRONIC RESPIRATORY DISEASES

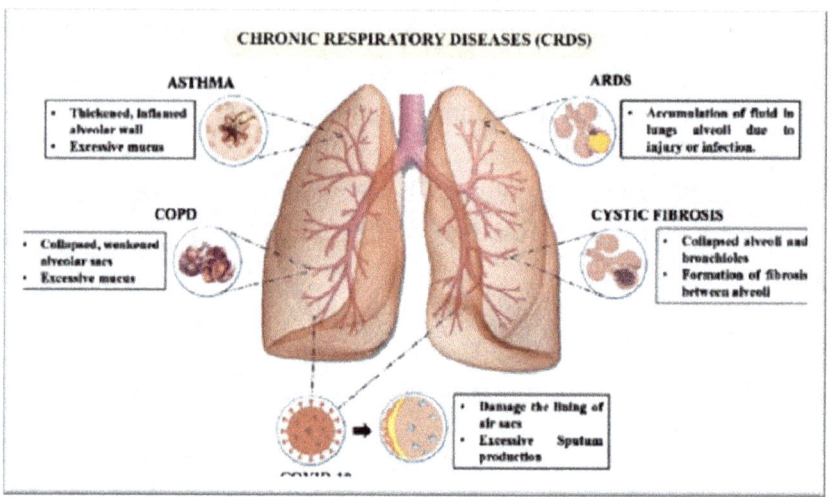

Chronic respiratory diseases, such as asthma, chronic obstructive pulmonary disease (COPD), and pulmonary fibrosis, pose significant health challenges due to their progressive nature and impact on quality of life. Recent advancements in treatment options are transforming the management of these conditions, offering new hope for patients and improving clinical outcomes. This lesson delves into the innovative therapies and approaches that are making a difference in the lives of those affected by chronic respiratory diseases.

Biologic Therapies

Biologic therapies have emerged as a groundbreaking treatment option for chronic respiratory diseases, particularly asthma and COPD. These therapies target specific components of the immune system involved in the inflammatory processes underlying these conditions.

- Monoclonal Antibodies (mAbs): Monoclonal antibodies are engineered proteins that target specific molecules involved in inflammation. For instance, omalizumab targets IgE antibodies, reducing allergic inflammation in patients with severe asthma. Other mAbs, such as mepolizumab, reslizumab, and benralizumab, target interleukin-5 (IL-5), a key cytokine in eosinophilic asthma.
- Dupilumab: Dupilumab is a biologic that targets the IL-4 and IL-13 pathways, which are implicated in both asthma and atopic dermatitis. It has shown significant efficacy in reducing asthma exacerbations and improving lung function in patients with moderate to severe asthma.
- Benralizumab: Benralizumab targets the IL-5 receptor on eosinophils, leading to their depletion. This results in reduced exacerbations and improved lung function in patients with eosinophilic asthma.

Gene Therapy

Gene therapy is an innovative approach that aims to correct or modify genetic defects underlying certain respiratory diseases. While still in the experimental stages, it holds great promise for the treatment of conditions such as cystic fibrosis and alpha-1 antitrypsin deficiency.

- Cystic Fibrosis: Cystic fibrosis is caused by mutations in the CFTR gene, leading to defective chloride ion transport and thick mucus production. Gene therapy approaches aim to deliver a functional copy of the CFTR gene to the airway epithelial cells. Early clinical trials have shown promising results, with improvements in lung function and reduction in respiratory infections.
- Alpha-1 Antitrypsin Deficiency: This genetic disorder leads to a deficiency of alpha-1 antitrypsin, a protein that protects the lungs from inflammation. Gene therapy strategies are being developed to deliver the gene encoding alpha-1 antitrypsin to the liver, where it can be produced and secreted into the bloodstream to reach the lungs.

Stem Cell Therapy

Stem cell therapy is a rapidly advancing field with potential applications in the treatment of chronic respiratory diseases. The ability of stem cells to differentiate into various cell types and promote tissue regeneration makes them an attractive option for repairing damaged lung tissue.

- Mesenchymal Stem Cells (MSCs): MSCs have shown promise in preclinical and early clinical studies for their anti-inflammatory and immunomodulatory properties. They can migrate to sites of inflammation, secrete growth factors, and promote tissue repair. Studies are ongoing to evaluate their efficacy in conditions such as COPD and pulmonary fibrosis.
- Induced Pluripotent Stem Cells (iPSCs): iPSCs are generated from adult cells and have the ability to differentiate into any cell type, including lung epithelial cells. Research is focused on using iPSCs to create lung tissue for transplantation or to model respiratory diseases in vitro for drug testing.

Targeted Drug Delivery Systems

Advancements in drug delivery systems are enhancing the efficacy and safety of treatments for chronic respiratory diseases. These systems aim to deliver medications directly to the lungs, reducing systemic side effects and improving therapeutic outcomes.

- Inhalation Therapies: Inhalation remains the primary mode of drug delivery for many respiratory diseases. Innovations in inhaler technology, such as smart inhalers, ensure optimal drug delivery and adherence. Smart inhalers can track usage, provide reminders, and connect to digital health platforms for remote monitoring.
- Nanoparticle-Based Delivery: Nanoparticles can be engineered to carry drugs directly to the lungs, improving drug solubility, stability, and bioavailability. This targeted approach can enhance the therapeutic effects of drugs while minimizing systemic exposure and side effects.

- Liposome-Based Delivery: Liposomes are spherical vesicles that can encapsulate drugs, protecting them from degradation and allowing for controlled release. Liposome-based inhalation therapies are being developed for conditions such as pulmonary fibrosis and lung cancer.

Lifestyle and Behavioral Interventions

In addition to pharmacological treatments, lifestyle and behavioral interventions play a crucial role in the management of chronic respiratory diseases. These interventions aim to reduce disease burden, improve quality of life, and enhance overall health.

- Pulmonary Rehabilitation: Pulmonary rehabilitation programs encompass exercise training, nutritional counseling, and education to improve physical fitness and respiratory function. These programs have been shown to reduce symptoms, enhance exercise tolerance, and improve quality of life in patients with COPD and other chronic respiratory diseases.
- Smoking Cessation Programs: Smoking is a major risk factor for many respiratory diseases, including COPD and lung cancer. Comprehensive smoking cessation programs that include behavioral counseling, pharmacotherapy, and support groups are essential for helping patients quit smoking and reduce disease progression.
- Nutritional Support: Proper nutrition is vital for maintaining lung health and overall well-being. Nutritional counseling can help patients achieve and maintain a healthy weight, reduce inflammation, and support immune function. Specific dietary interventions, such as high-protein diets, may be beneficial for patients with COPD to maintain muscle mass and strength.

The landscape of treatment for chronic respiratory diseases is rapidly evolving, with innovative therapies offering new hope for patients and transforming clinical practice. Biologic therapies, gene therapy, stem cell therapy, targeted drug delivery systems, and lifestyle interventions are at the forefront of this transformation, providing more effective and personalized treatment options. As research and technology continue to advance, the future holds even greater promise for improving the management and outcomes of chronic respiratory diseases.

DISCUSSION QUESTIONS

- How have therapeutic approaches in respiratory medicine evolved, and what are some of the most promising therapies for respiratory diseases currently in development or under investigation?
- What role do patient-centric approaches, such as personalized medicine and precision therapies, play in optimizing treatment outcomes for patients with respiratory diseases, and how can healthcare providers integrate these approaches into clinical practice?

LESSON TWO: EMERGING TECHNOLOGIES IN RESPIRATORY CARE

The field of respiratory care is experiencing a technological revolution, with emerging technologies poised to transform the way respiratory diseases are diagnosed, treated, and managed. These innovations are enhancing precision, efficiency, and patient outcomes, offering new tools for healthcare providers and patients alike. This lesson delves into the latest technological advancements in respiratory care, exploring their applications, benefits, and potential to reshape the future of respiratory medicine.

Artificial Intelligence and Machine Learning

Artificial intelligence (AI) and machine learning (ML) are at the forefront of technological advancements in respiratory care, offering capabilities that enhance diagnostic accuracy, treatment planning, and patient management.

- AI-Enhanced Imaging: AI algorithms are being developed to analyze medical imaging data, such as chest X-rays and CT scans, with high accuracy. These systems can detect abnormalities, quantify disease severity, and provide diagnostic suggestions, assisting radiologists and clinicians in making more informed decisions. For example, AI can help identify early signs of lung cancer or interstitial lung disease, improving early detection and treatment outcomes.

- Predictive Analytics: ML models can analyze large datasets from electronic health records (EHRs) to identify patterns and predict disease progression and outcomes. Predictive analytics can help healthcare providers identify patients at high risk of respiratory complications, enabling proactive interventions and personalized care plans.
- Automated Spirometry Interpretation: AI-based systems can automate the interpretation of spirometry results, identifying patterns indicative of specific respiratory diseases. This automation ensures consistent and accurate assessments, reducing the potential for human error and streamlining the diagnostic process.

Telemedicine and Remote Monitoring

The integration of telemedicine and remote monitoring technologies has revolutionized respiratory care, particularly in the context of the COVID-19 pandemic. These tools enable continuous monitoring, timely interventions, and improved access to care.

- Remote Patient Monitoring (RPM): RPM systems use connected devices, such as spirometers, pulse oximeters, and wearable sensors, to monitor patients' respiratory parameters in real time. Data is transmitted to healthcare providers, allowing for continuous assessment and timely interventions. RPM has been shown to reduce hospitalizations, improve disease management, and enhance patient outcomes in conditions such as asthma and COPD.
- Telehealth Consultations: Telehealth platforms enable virtual consultations between patients and healthcare providers, expanding access to specialist care, particularly in remote and underserved areas. Telehealth has been instrumental in

managing chronic respiratory diseases during the COVID-19 pandemic, reducing the need for in-person visits and minimizing exposure risks.
- Digital Health Platforms: Comprehensive digital health platforms integrate telemedicine, remote monitoring, and patient education, providing a holistic approach to respiratory care. These platforms facilitate communication between patients and providers, support medication adherence, and offer personalized health insights.

Wearable Technology

Wearable technology is playing an increasingly important role in respiratory care, offering continuous monitoring and real-time feedback on respiratory health.

- Wearable Spirometers: Portable spirometers that can be worn or carried by patients allow for frequent lung function testing outside of clinical settings. These devices provide real-time data on respiratory parameters, enabling patients to monitor their condition and share data with their healthcare providers.
- Smart Inhalers: Smart inhalers are equipped with sensors that track medication usage and provide reminders and feedback to patients. These devices ensure optimal medication adherence and help healthcare providers monitor treatment effectiveness and adjust therapy as needed.
- Wearable Pulse Oximeters: Wearable pulse oximeters continuously monitor blood oxygen levels and heart rate, providing valuable data for managing conditions such as COPD and sleep apnea. These devices can alert patients and providers to significant changes in oxygen saturation, prompting timely interventions.

Robotics and Automation

Robotic technologies and automation are enhancing the precision and efficiency of respiratory care procedures, reducing the risk of complications and improving patient outcomes.

- Robotic-Assisted Bronchoscopy: Robotic-assisted bronchoscopy systems, such as the Monarch™ Platform, offer enhanced visualization and maneuverability, allowing for precise navigation to peripheral lung lesions. These systems improve the accuracy of biopsies and the diagnosis of early-stage lung cancer.
- Automated Ventilation Systems: Advanced mechanical ventilators with automated features and AI-driven algorithms can adjust ventilation parameters in real time based on patient needs. These systems optimize respiratory support, reduce the risk of ventilator-associated complications, and improve patient outcomes in critical care settings.
- Automated Drug Delivery: Automated drug delivery systems, such as nebulizers and inhalers with smart features, ensure accurate dosing and adherence to prescribed treatments. These systems can adjust medication delivery based on real-time respiratory parameters, enhancing treatment efficacy.

3D Printing and Personalized Medicine

3D printing technology is revolutionizing personalized medicine in respiratory care, enabling the creation of customized medical devices and implants tailored to individual patient needs.

- 3D-Printed Airway Stents: 3D printing allows for the creation of personalized airway stents that match the unique anatomy of a patient's airways. These custom stents can improve the management of conditions such as tracheomalacia and airway stenosis, reducing complications and enhancing patient comfort.
- Custom Prosthetics and Implants: 3D printing is also used to create custom prosthetics and implants for patients with

respiratory conditions requiring surgical interventions. These personalized devices offer better fit, function, and integration with the patient's anatomy.

The emergence of new technologies in respiratory care is transforming the landscape of diagnosis, treatment, and patient management. AI and ML, telemedicine, wearable technology, robotics, and 3D printing are just a few of the innovations driving this transformation. As these technologies continue to evolve and integrate into clinical practice, they promise to enhance precision, efficiency, and patient outcomes, ultimately revolutionizing respiratory care.

DISCUSSION QUESTIONS

- What are some of the emerging technologies for respiratory monitoring and management, and how do these innovations empower patients to take a more active role in managing their respiratory health?
- How can healthcare providers leverage telemedicine and remote monitoring technologies to improve access to care for patients with respiratory diseases, particularly in underserved or remote communities?

MODULE THREE

LESSON ONE: TELEMEDICINE AND REMOTE MONITORING IN RESPIRATORY MEDICINE

The integration of telemedicine and remote monitoring technologies has become a cornerstone of modern respiratory medicine, particularly in response to the challenges posed by the COVID-19 pandemic. These innovations are enhancing access to care, enabling continuous monitoring, and improving patient outcomes. This lesson explores the role of telemedicine and remote monitoring in respiratory medicine, highlighting their applications, benefits, and impact on patient care.

Telemedicine in Respiratory Care

Telemedicine involves the use of digital communication technologies to provide healthcare services remotely. In respiratory medicine, telemedicine has become an essential tool for delivering care to patients, particularly those in remote or underserved areas.

- Virtual Consultations: Telemedicine platforms enable virtual consultations between patients and healthcare providers, facilitating timely diagnosis, treatment, and follow-up care. These consultations can include video calls, phone calls, and secure messaging, allowing for flexible and convenient interactions.
- Specialist Access: Telemedicine expands access to respiratory specialists, particularly in regions with limited healthcare resources. Patients can receive expert opinions, second opinions, and specialized care without the need to travel long distances.
- Chronic Disease Management: Telemedicine is particularly valuable for managing chronic respiratory diseases such as asthma, COPD, and pulmonary fibrosis. Regular virtual check-ins allow healthcare providers to monitor disease progression, adjust treatment plans, and provide ongoing support.

Remote Patient Monitoring (RPM)

Remote patient monitoring involves the use of connected devices to track patients' health parameters in real time, providing continuous data to healthcare providers for proactive management.

- Connected Devices: RPM systems utilize a variety of connected devices, including spirometers, pulse oximeters, and wearable sensors, to monitor respiratory parameters such as lung function, oxygen saturation, and respiratory rate. These devices transmit data to healthcare providers, enabling continuous assessment and timely interventions.
- Data Analytics: RPM platforms often incorporate data analytics to process and interpret the large volumes of data collected. These analytics can identify trends, detect early signs of deterioration, and trigger alerts for healthcare providers to take action.
- Patient Engagement: RPM enhances patient engagement by empowering individuals to actively participate in their own

care. Patients can track their health metrics, receive real-time feedback, and adhere to personalized care plans.

Benefits of Telemedicine and Remote Monitoring

The integration of telemedicine and remote monitoring offers numerous benefits for both patients and healthcare providers, improving the overall quality of respiratory care.

- Improved Access to Care: Telemedicine and RPM expand access to care, particularly for patients in rural or underserved areas. Patients can receive timely medical attention without the need for travel, reducing barriers to care.
- Enhanced Monitoring and Early Intervention: Continuous monitoring through RPM allows for the early detection of exacerbations or complications, enabling prompt interventions and preventing hospitalizations. This proactive approach improves patient outcomes and reduces healthcare costs.
- Convenience and Flexibility: Telemedicine offers convenience and flexibility for patients, allowing them to schedule consultations and receive care from the comfort of their homes. This is particularly beneficial for individuals with mobility issues or those requiring frequent follow-ups.
- Reduced Exposure Risk: During the COVID-19 pandemic, telemedicine has played a critical role in reducing the risk of exposure to the virus by minimizing the need for in-person visits. This has been especially important for patients with chronic respiratory conditions who are at higher risk of severe illness.
- Personalized Care: Telemedicine and RPM enable personalized care plans tailored to individual patient needs. Healthcare providers can adjust treatments based on real-time data, ensuring that patients receive the most appropriate and effective interventions.

Challenges and Considerations

While telemedicine and remote monitoring offer significant benefits, there are also challenges and considerations that must be addressed to ensure their successful implementation.

- Technology Access and Literacy: Access to the necessary technology and digital literacy can be barriers for some patients, particularly the elderly or those in low-income communities. Efforts must be made to ensure equitable access and provide education and support for using telemedicine tools.
- Data Security and Privacy: The transmission and storage of health data through telemedicine and RPM platforms raise concerns about data security and privacy. Robust security measures and compliance with regulations such as HIPAA are essential to protect patient information.
- Reimbursement and Regulation: Reimbursement policies and regulatory frameworks for telemedicine and RPM vary by region and can impact the adoption and sustainability of these services. Advocacy and policy development are needed to ensure appropriate reimbursement and regulatory support.
- Integration with Traditional Care: Telemedicine and RPM should be integrated with traditional in-person care to provide a comprehensive approach to patient management. Hybrid models that combine virtual and in-person visits can offer the best of both worlds.

Telemedicine and remote monitoring are transforming respiratory medicine, offering new ways to deliver care, enhance patient engagement, and improve outcomes. These technologies have become essential tools in the management of respiratory diseases, particularly during the COVID-19 pandemic. As telemedicine and RPM continue to evolve and integrate into clinical practice, they hold the potential to further revolutionize respiratory care, making it more accessible, efficient, and patient-centered.

DISCUSSION QUESTIONS

- What are the key principles of precision medicine in the context of respiratory oncology, and how do these approaches enhance diagnosis, treatment selection, and patient outcomes?
- What challenges exist in implementing precision medicine approaches in respiratory oncology, and how can healthcare providers overcome these challenges to ensure broader adoption and impact?

LESSON TWO: PERSONALIZED MEDICINE IN RESPIRATORY CARE

Personalized medicine is revolutionizing respiratory care by tailoring treatments to individual patients based on their genetic, molecular, and clinical profiles. This approach aims to improve the efficacy of treatments, reduce adverse effects, and enhance patient outcomes. In this lesson, we will explore the role of personalized medicine in respiratory care, focusing on how genetic and molecular insights are driving more targeted and effective treatments.

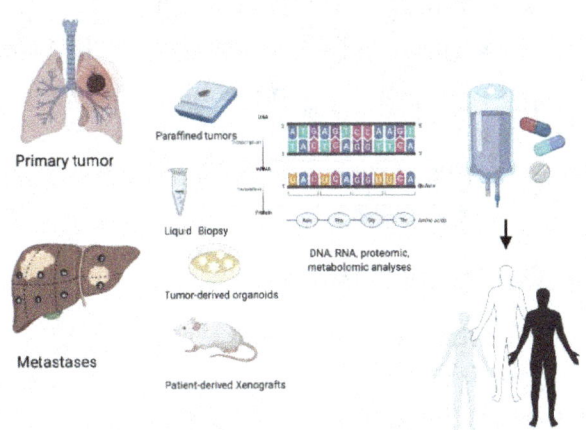

Genetic Insights and Targeted Therapies

Advancements in genetic research have uncovered the genetic underpinnings of many respiratory diseases, paving the way for targeted therapies that address the specific molecular causes of these conditions.

- Genetic Testing: Genetic testing can identify mutations and variations associated with respiratory diseases, such as cystic fibrosis (CF), alpha-1 antitrypsin deficiency, and primary ciliary dyskinesia. These insights enable early diagnosis, risk assessment, and personalized treatment plans.
- Targeted Therapies for CF: Cystic fibrosis is caused by mutations in the CFTR gene. Targeted therapies, such as CFTR modulators, are designed to correct the defective protein produced by these mutations. Drugs like ivacaftor,

lumacaftor, and elexacaftor have shown significant benefits in improving lung function and reducing pulmonary exacerbations in CF patients with specific mutations.
- Alpha-1 Antitrypsin Replacement Therapy: Alpha-1 antitrypsin deficiency is a genetic disorder that leads to a lack of a protein protecting the lungs from inflammation. Replacement therapy with alpha-1 antitrypsin can slow disease progression and improve lung function in affected individuals.

Molecular Biomarkers

The identification of molecular biomarkers has revolutionized the diagnosis and management of respiratory diseases, enabling more precise and individualized treatments.

- Biomarkers in Asthma: Biomarkers such as blood eosinophil count, serum IgE levels, and fractional exhaled nitric oxide (FeNO) are used to phenotype asthma and guide the use of targeted therapies. For instance, patients with high eosinophil counts may benefit from biologics targeting IL-5, such as mepolizumab or benralizumab.
- Biomarkers in Lung Cancer: Liquid biopsy, which analyzes circulating tumor DNA (ctDNA) in blood samples, offers a non-invasive method for detecting genetic mutations in lung cancer. This technique can identify actionable mutations, such as EGFR or ALK rearrangements, guiding the use of targeted therapies and monitoring treatment response.
- Biomarkers in Pulmonary Fibrosis: In pulmonary fibrosis, biomarkers such as serum surfactant proteins and KL-6 levels can provide insights into disease activity and prognosis. These markers help in monitoring disease progression and evaluating the efficacy of antifibrotic therapies.

Pharmacogenomics

Pharmacogenomics studies how genetic variations affect individual responses to drugs, allowing for the optimization of drug therapy based on a patient's genetic profile.

- Asthma Pharmacogenomics: Genetic variations can influence the response to asthma medications, such as beta-agonists and corticosteroids. For example, polymorphisms in the ADRB2 gene can affect the efficacy of beta-agonists, guiding personalized asthma management.
- COPD Pharmacogenomics: Genetic factors can also impact the response to COPD treatments. Variations in genes related to the metabolism of bronchodilators and anti-inflammatory drugs can influence treatment efficacy and adverse effects, allowing for personalized COPD therapy.

Precision Medicine Initiatives

Precision medicine initiatives are integrating genetic, molecular, and clinical data to develop personalized treatment approaches for respiratory diseases.

- The Precision Medicine Initiative (PMI): Launched by the National Institutes of Health (NIH), the PMI aims to advance precision medicine through research and the development of personalized treatments. This initiative includes the All of Us Research Program, which collects health data from diverse populations to understand how genetic and environmental factors influence health and disease.
- The National Heart, Lung, and Blood Institute (NHLBI) Precision Medicine Activities: NHLBI is conducting research to identify genetic and molecular factors associated with respiratory diseases, with the goal of developing targeted therapies and improving patient outcomes.

Challenges and Future Directions

While personalized medicine holds great promise for respiratory care, several challenges must be addressed to fully realize its potential.

- Access to Genetic Testing: Access to genetic testing and personalized treatments can be limited by cost, availability, and healthcare disparities. Efforts are needed to ensure equitable access to these technologies and therapies.
- Integration into Clinical Practice: Integrating genetic and molecular insights into routine clinical practice requires education and training for healthcare providers, as well as the development of standardized guidelines and protocols.
- Ethical and Privacy Considerations: The use of genetic data raises ethical and privacy concerns, including issues related to data security, informed consent, and potential discrimination. Robust policies and regulations are needed to address these concerns.

Personalized medicine is transforming respiratory care by providing more targeted and effective treatments based on individual genetic and molecular profiles. Genetic insights, molecular biomarkers, pharmacogenomics, and precision medicine initiatives are driving this transformation, offering new hope for patients with respiratory diseases. As research and technology continue to advance, personalized medicine promises to further enhance the precision and efficacy of respiratory care, ultimately improving patient outcomes.

DISCUSSION QUESTIONS

- What are the key components of respiratory rehabilitation and pulmonary rehabilitation programs, and how do these interventions improve respiratory function, exercise tolerance, and quality of life for patients with chronic respiratory diseases?
- How can innovations in technology, such as virtual reality and gamification, enhance the delivery and effectiveness of

respiratory rehabilitation programs, particularly in engaging patients and promoting adherence to treatment regimens?

MODULE FOUR

LESSON ONE: LIFESTYLE AND BEHAVIORAL INTERVENTIONS IN RESPIRATORY HEALTH

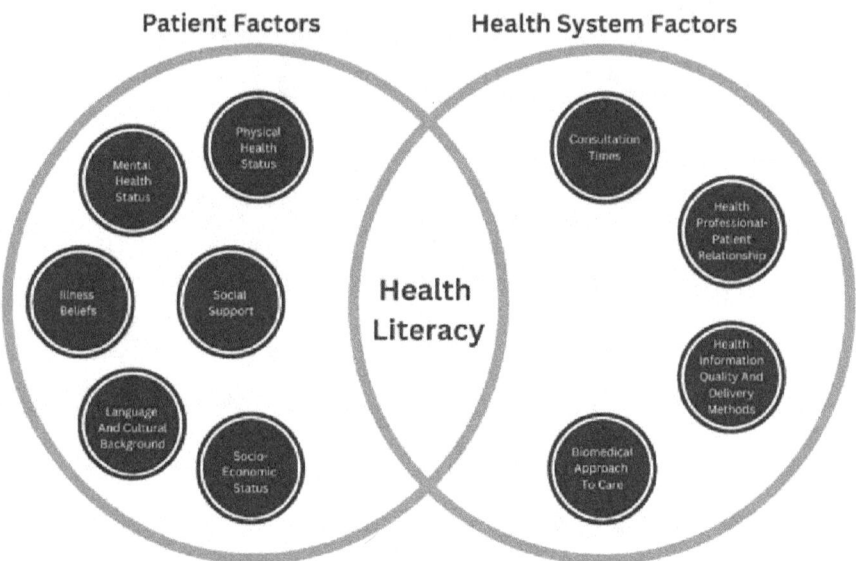

Lifestyle and behavioral interventions play a crucial role in the management and prevention of respiratory diseases. These interventions can complement medical treatments, improve quality of life, and enhance overall respiratory health. This lesson explores the impact of lifestyle and behavioral changes on respiratory health, highlighting effective strategies and their benefits.

Smoking Cessation

Smoking is a major risk factor for many respiratory diseases, including chronic obstructive pulmonary disease (COPD), lung cancer, and asthma. Quitting smoking is one of the most effective interventions for improving respiratory health and reducing disease progression.

- Behavioral Counseling: Behavioral counseling provides support and strategies to help individuals quit smoking.

Techniques such as motivational interviewing, cognitive-behavioral therapy (CBT), and support groups can increase the likelihood of successful smoking cessation.
- Pharmacotherapy: Medications such as nicotine replacement therapy (NRT), bupropion, and varenicline can aid in smoking cessation by reducing withdrawal symptoms and cravings. Combining pharmacotherapy with behavioral counseling is often more effective than either approach alone.
- Digital Interventions: Digital tools, such as mobile apps and online programs, offer accessible and personalized support for smoking cessation. These tools can provide educational resources, track progress, and offer reminders and encouragement.

Physical Activity

Regular physical activity is beneficial for respiratory health, improving lung function, reducing symptoms, and enhancing overall well-being.

- Exercise Training: Exercise training is a core component of pulmonary rehabilitation programs for patients with chronic respiratory diseases. Activities such as aerobic exercise, strength training, and flexibility exercises can improve exercise tolerance, reduce dyspnea, and enhance quality of life.
- Breathing Exercises: Breathing exercises, such as diaphragmatic breathing and pursed-lip breathing, can help improve lung function and reduce breathlessness in patients with COPD and asthma. These exercises focus on optimizing breathing patterns and increasing lung capacity.
- Outdoor Activities: Engaging in outdoor activities, such as walking, hiking, and cycling, can provide both physical and mental health benefits. Exposure to nature and fresh air can improve mood, reduce stress, and enhance respiratory function.

Nutrition and Diet

Proper nutrition is essential for maintaining lung health and supporting overall well-being. Certain dietary interventions can have specific benefits for respiratory health.

- Anti-Inflammatory Diet: An anti-inflammatory diet rich in fruits, vegetables, whole grains, and healthy fats can help reduce inflammation and oxidative stress in the lungs. Nutrients such as omega-3 fatty acids, antioxidants, and vitamins C and E are particularly beneficial.
- Weight Management: Maintaining a healthy weight is important for respiratory health, as obesity can exacerbate symptoms of respiratory diseases and increase the risk of complications. Nutritional counseling can help patients achieve and maintain a healthy weight through balanced diet and portion control.
- Hydration: Adequate hydration is important for maintaining the health of the respiratory tract and facilitating the clearance of mucus. Drinking enough water and consuming hydrating foods, such as fruits and vegetables, can support respiratory function.

Environmental Modifications

Modifying the home and work environment can help reduce exposure to respiratory irritants and allergens, improving respiratory health and reducing symptoms.

- Indoor Air Quality: Improving indoor air quality by reducing exposure to pollutants, allergens, and irritants is crucial for respiratory health. Measures such as using air purifiers, reducing the use of chemical cleaners, and controlling humidity levels can help improve indoor air quality.
- Allergen Avoidance: For individuals with respiratory allergies, avoiding exposure to allergens such as dust mites, pet dander, and pollen is important. Strategies include using

allergen-proof bedding, keeping pets out of bedrooms, and regularly cleaning and dusting the home.
- Occupational Health: For individuals working in environments with respiratory hazards, occupational health measures such as using protective equipment, following safety protocols, and ensuring proper ventilation can reduce the risk of respiratory issues.

Stress Management

Chronic stress can negatively impact respiratory health by exacerbating symptoms and triggering exacerbations of respiratory diseases. Effective stress management techniques can improve respiratory outcomes and overall well-being.

- Relaxation Techniques: Relaxation techniques such as deep breathing, progressive muscle relaxation, and guided imagery can help reduce stress and improve respiratory function. These techniques can be incorporated into daily routines to promote relaxation and well-being.
- Mindfulness and Meditation: Mindfulness and meditation practices can help individuals manage stress and anxiety, improving respiratory symptoms and overall quality of life. Techniques such as mindfulness-based stress reduction (MBSR) and mindful breathing can be particularly beneficial.
- Counseling and Support: Counseling and support groups can provide emotional support and coping strategies for individuals with chronic respiratory diseases. These resources can help patients manage stress, anxiety, and depression, improving their overall well-being.

Lifestyle and behavioral interventions play a vital role in respiratory health, offering effective strategies for preventing and managing respiratory diseases. Smoking cessation, physical activity, nutrition, environmental modifications, and stress management are key components of a holistic approach to respiratory care. By incorporating these interventions into their daily lives, individuals can improve their respiratory function, reduce symptoms, and enhance their overall quality of life.

DISCUSSION QUESTIONS

- What are the environmental factors that impact respiratory health, and how can individuals and communities mitigate these influences to reduce the risk of respiratory diseases and improve lung function?
- How do climate change and environmental degradation affect respiratory health on a global scale, and what collaborative efforts are needed to address these challenges and protect vulnerable populations?

MODULE FIVE

LESSON ONE: FUTURE DIRECTIONS IN RESPIRATORY MEDICINE

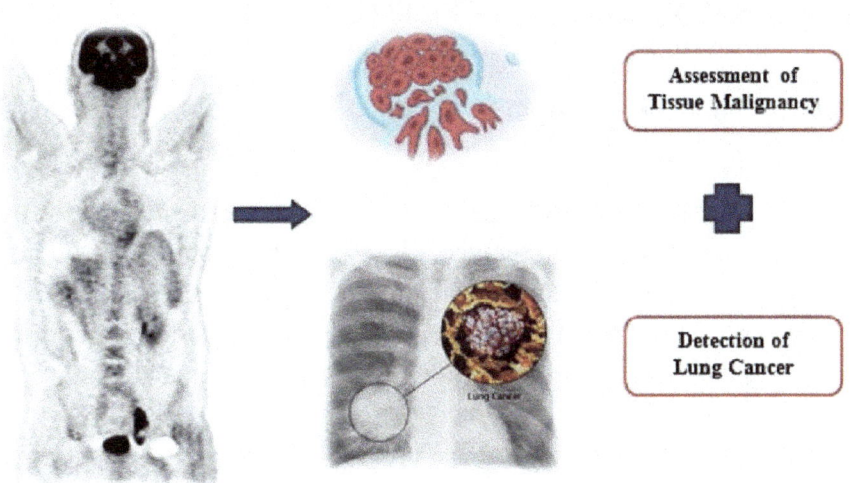

The field of respiratory medicine is continuously evolving, driven by advances in research, technology, and clinical practice. This lesson summarizes the key insights and advancements discussed in previous lesson and explores future directions in respiratory medicine, highlighting the potential for further improving respiratory health.

Advancements in Diagnostics and Treatment

- Precision Medicine: The integration of genetic, molecular, and clinical data will continue to drive the development of personalized treatments, improving the efficacy and safety of therapies for respiratory diseases. Advancements in genetic testing, biomarker discovery, and pharmacogenomics will enhance our ability to tailor treatments to individual patients.
- Innovative Therapies: Emerging therapies such as biologics, gene therapy, and stem cell therapy hold great promise for treating chronic respiratory diseases. Ongoing research and

clinical trials will expand our understanding of these therapies and their potential to transform patient outcomes.
- AI and Machine Learning: The use of AI and machine learning in respiratory medicine will enhance diagnostic accuracy, predictive analytics, and treatment planning. These technologies will enable more precise and efficient care, improving patient outcomes and reducing healthcare costs.

Technological Innovations

- Telemedicine and RPM: The continued integration of telemedicine and remote patient monitoring will improve access to care, enhance disease management, and support personalized treatment plans. The expansion of digital health platforms will facilitate communication between patients and providers, promoting patient engagement and adherence to care plans.
- Wearable Technology: Wearable devices will play an increasingly important role in respiratory care, offering continuous monitoring and real-time feedback on respiratory health. Advances in sensor technology and data analytics will enhance the capabilities of wearable devices, providing valuable insights for patients and healthcare providers.
- Robotics and Automation: Robotic technologies and automation will enhance the precision and efficiency of respiratory care procedures, reducing the risk of complications and improving patient outcomes. Innovations in robotic-assisted bronchoscopy, automated ventilation systems, and drug delivery will further advance the field.

Public Health and Prevention

- Smoking Cessation Programs: Comprehensive smoking cessation programs will continue to be a cornerstone of respiratory health, reducing the burden of smoking-related diseases. Expanding access to smoking cessation resources

and integrating digital tools will support individuals in quitting smoking and maintaining long-term abstinence.
- Environmental Health: Efforts to improve indoor and outdoor air quality will have a significant impact on respiratory health. Policies and initiatives aimed at reducing pollution, controlling allergens, and promoting clean air will help prevent respiratory diseases and improve overall public health.
- Health Education: Public health campaigns and educational programs will play a crucial role in raising awareness about respiratory health and promoting healthy behaviors. Empowering individuals with knowledge about risk factors, prevention strategies, and early detection will support proactive health management.

Future Research and Collaboration

- Collaborative Research: Collaborative research efforts, including multi-center studies and international partnerships, will accelerate the discovery of new treatments and interventions for respiratory diseases. Sharing data and resources across institutions and countries will enhance our understanding of respiratory health and disease.
- Patient-Centered Research: Engaging patients in research and incorporating their perspectives will ensure that advancements in respiratory medicine align with patient needs and preferences. Patient-centered research will enhance the relevance and impact of scientific discoveries, improving the quality of care and patient outcomes.
- Longitudinal Studies: Long-term studies that track patients over time will provide valuable insights into the natural history of respiratory diseases, the long-term effects of treatments, and the factors influencing disease progression and outcomes. These studies will inform the development of more effective and sustainable care strategies.

The future of respiratory medicine holds great promise, with advancements in diagnostics, treatment, technology, public health, and research paving the way for improved respiratory health. By embracing innovation, fostering collaboration, and prioritizing patient-centered care, we can continue to advance the field and enhance the lives of individuals with respiratory diseases.

DISCUSSION QUESTIONS

- What are some of the most promising future directions in respiratory medicine, and how might advancements in technology, research, and clinical practice shape the landscape of respiratory care in the coming years?
- What are the ethical considerations and societal implications of future developments in respiratory medicine, and how can healthcare providers, researchers, policymakers, and the public collaborate to ensure that innovation in respiratory care is ethically sound and socially responsible?

MODULE SIX

LESSON ONE: THE ROLE OF ARTIFICIAL INTELLIGENCE IN RESPIRATORY MEDICINE

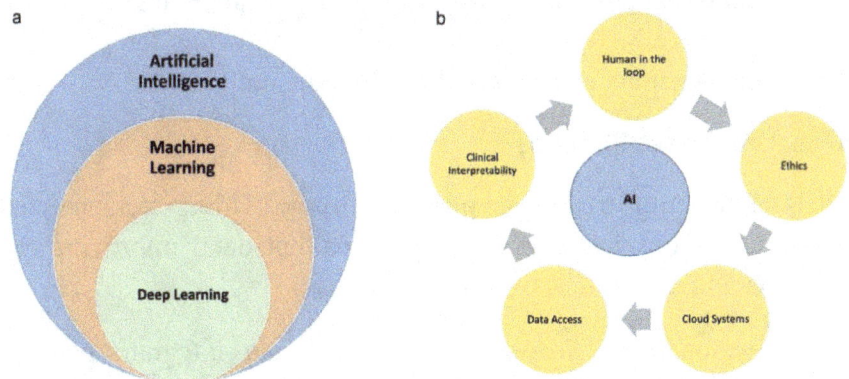

Artificial Intelligence (AI) is transforming the landscape of respiratory medicine by enhancing diagnostic accuracy, streamlining treatment processes, and enabling personalized care. This lesson delves into the various applications of AI in respiratory medicine, exploring its current uses, potential benefits, and the challenges associated with its integration.

AI in Diagnostics

AI technologies, particularly machine learning and deep learning, are revolutionizing diagnostic procedures by enabling rapid, accurate, and non-invasive assessments.

- Imaging Analysis: AI algorithms can analyze medical images such as X-rays, CT scans, and MRIs with high precision, identifying abnormalities that might be missed by the human eye. For example, AI can detect early signs of lung cancer, pulmonary nodules, and interstitial lung diseases, facilitating timely intervention.
- Pattern Recognition: AI systems excel at recognizing patterns in complex datasets. In respiratory medicine, AI can analyze

spirometry data, sleep studies, and electronic health records to diagnose conditions like asthma, COPD, and sleep apnea more efficiently.
- Predictive Analytics: AI can predict disease progression and patient outcomes by analyzing historical data and identifying trends. For instance, predictive models can estimate the risk of exacerbations in COPD patients, allowing for proactive management and personalized treatment plans.

AI in Treatment Planning

AI is enhancing treatment planning by providing personalized recommendations based on individual patient data, improving the precision and effectiveness of interventions.

- Personalized Treatment Plans: AI can integrate genetic, clinical, and lifestyle data to create personalized treatment plans for patients with respiratory diseases. By considering unique patient profiles, AI helps optimize medication regimens, identify the most effective therapies, and minimize adverse effects.
- Drug Development: AI accelerates drug discovery and development by predicting the efficacy and safety of new compounds. Machine learning models can analyze vast amounts of data to identify potential drug candidates for respiratory diseases, reducing the time and cost associated with traditional drug development processes.
- Robotic Assistance: In surgical procedures such as lung biopsies and thoracic surgeries, AI-powered robotic systems enhance precision and reduce complications. These systems can assist surgeons in navigating complex anatomical structures and performing minimally invasive procedures with greater accuracy.

Patient Monitoring and Management

AI plays a crucial role in remote patient monitoring and chronic disease management, improving patient engagement and outcomes.

- Remote Monitoring: AI-powered wearable devices and sensors continuously monitor patients' vital signs, respiratory parameters, and activity levels. These devices can detect early signs of deterioration and alert healthcare providers, enabling timely interventions and reducing hospitalizations.
- Virtual Health Assistants: AI-driven virtual assistants can provide patients with personalized health advice, medication reminders, and symptom tracking. These assistants enhance patient engagement, adherence to treatment plans, and self-management of chronic respiratory conditions.
- Telemedicine Integration: AI integrates with telemedicine platforms to provide real-time analytics and decision support during virtual consultations. By analyzing patient data, AI can assist healthcare providers in diagnosing conditions, recommending treatments, and monitoring progress remotely.

Challenges and Ethical Considerations

Despite its potential, the integration of AI in respiratory medicine faces several challenges and ethical considerations that must be addressed to ensure its successful implementation.

- Data Quality and Bias: AI algorithms require high-quality, diverse data to function accurately. Biases in data collection and algorithm development can lead to disparities in healthcare outcomes. Ensuring representative datasets and addressing algorithmic bias are critical for equitable AI applications.
- Privacy and Security: The use of AI involves handling large volumes of sensitive patient data, raising concerns about privacy and security. Robust data protection measures and compliance with regulations such as HIPAA are essential to safeguard patient information.
- Clinical Integration: Integrating AI into clinical workflows requires careful planning and collaboration between technology developers and healthcare providers. Training healthcare professionals to effectively use AI tools and

ensuring seamless integration with existing systems are necessary for successful adoption.
- Regulatory Approval: The regulatory landscape for AI in healthcare is still evolving. Gaining regulatory approval for AI-based medical devices and algorithms involves rigorous validation and testing to ensure safety, efficacy, and reliability.

Future Directions

The future of AI in respiratory medicine holds exciting possibilities, with ongoing research and development paving the way for more advanced and sophisticated applications.

- Enhanced Predictive Models: Continued advancements in machine learning will improve the accuracy and reliability of predictive models, enabling more precise risk assessment and early intervention for respiratory diseases.
- AI and Genomics: Integrating AI with genomic data will enhance our understanding of the genetic basis of respiratory diseases, leading to more targeted and personalized treatments.
- AI-Driven Clinical Trials: AI can optimize the design and execution of clinical trials, accelerating the development of new therapies for respiratory diseases. By identifying suitable candidates and predicting treatment responses, AI can improve trial efficiency and outcomes.
- Global Health Impact: AI has the potential to address global health challenges by providing scalable solutions for respiratory disease management in resource-limited settings. Telemedicine and AI-driven diagnostic tools can improve access to care and reduce healthcare disparities worldwide.

AI is poised to revolutionize respiratory medicine, offering innovative solutions for diagnosis, treatment, and patient management. By harnessing the power of AI, healthcare providers can deliver more precise, efficient, and personalized care, ultimately improving respiratory health outcomes. As we continue to explore and integrate AI technologies, it is essential to address the associated challenges and ethical considerations to ensure that these advancements benefit all patients.

DISCUSSION QUESTIONS

- How can healthcare providers harness the potential of artificial intelligence to augment clinical decision-making and improve patient outcomes in respiratory medicine, while maintaining patient trust and ensuring the ethical use of AI technologies?
- What are the challenges and limitations of integrating artificial intelligence into respiratory medicine, and how can healthcare organizations address concerns related to algorithmic bias, data privacy, and professional autonomy to maximize the benefits of AI while minimizing risks?

MODULE SEVEN

LESSON ONE: THE IMPORTANCE OF INTERDISCIPLINARY COLLABORATION IN RESPIRATORY MEDICINE

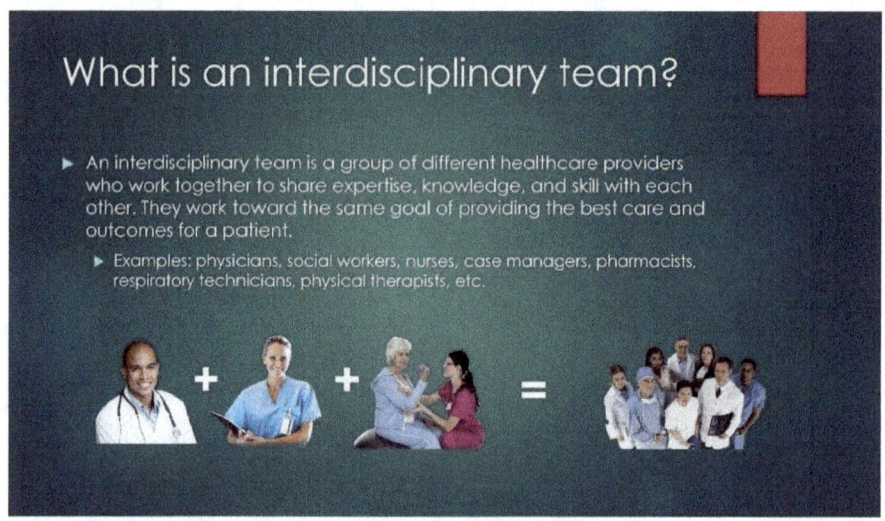

Interdisciplinary collaboration is essential in advancing respiratory medicine, as it brings together diverse expertise, perspectives, and resources to tackle complex health challenges. This lesson explores the importance of interdisciplinary teamwork in respiratory medicine, highlighting how collaborative efforts drive innovation, enhance patient care, and improve health outcomes.

The Role of Interdisciplinary Teams

Interdisciplinary teams in respiratory medicine consist of healthcare professionals from various specialties working together to provide comprehensive care for patients with respiratory diseases.

- Pulmonologists and Respiratory Therapists: Pulmonologists diagnose and manage respiratory conditions, while respiratory therapists provide specialized care, including breathing treatments, mechanical ventilation, and patient education.

Collaboration between these professionals ensures optimal management of respiratory diseases.

- Primary Care Physicians and Specialists: Primary care physicians play a crucial role in the early detection and management of respiratory diseases. Collaboration with specialists such as allergists, immunologists, and thoracic surgeons facilitates timely referrals, accurate diagnoses, and coordinated care.
- Nurses and Nurse Practitioners: Nurses and nurse practitioners provide essential patient care, education, and support. They work closely with other team members to implement treatment plans, monitor patient progress, and address patient concerns, contributing to improved outcomes and patient satisfaction.
- Pharmacists: Pharmacists offer valuable expertise in medication management, ensuring appropriate drug selection, dosing, and monitoring. They collaborate with the healthcare team to optimize pharmacotherapy and manage potential drug interactions and side effects.
- Dietitians and Nutritionists: Dietitians and nutritionists provide dietary guidance and support to patients with respiratory diseases. They work with the healthcare team to develop nutrition plans that enhance lung health, manage weight, and improve overall well-being.
- Physical Therapists and Exercise Physiologists: Physical therapists and exercise physiologists design and implement exercise programs for patients with respiratory conditions. They collaborate with the healthcare team to improve patients' physical fitness, lung function, and quality of life through tailored exercise interventions.
- Social Workers and Psychologists: Social workers and psychologists address the psychosocial aspects of respiratory care, providing emotional support, counseling, and resources for patients and their families. Their involvement helps

patients cope with the challenges of chronic respiratory diseases and improves adherence to treatment plans.

Benefits of Interdisciplinary Collaboration

Interdisciplinary collaboration offers numerous benefits for both patients and healthcare providers, enhancing the quality and effectiveness of respiratory care.

- Comprehensive Care: Collaborative efforts ensure that all aspects of a patient's health are addressed, from medical treatment to psychosocial support. This holistic approach improves patient outcomes and quality of life.
- Improved Communication: Interdisciplinary teams foster open communication and information-sharing among healthcare providers. This enhances coordination, reduces errors, and ensures that all team members are aligned in their efforts to provide optimal care.
- Enhanced Problem-Solving: Diverse expertise and perspectives contribute to innovative problem-solving and decision-making. Interdisciplinary collaboration allows healthcare providers to develop creative solutions to complex clinical challenges.
- Efficient Resource Utilization: Collaborative care optimizes the use of healthcare resources, reducing duplication of services and improving efficiency. This leads to cost savings and better allocation of resources to meet patient needs.
- Patient-Centered Care: Interdisciplinary teams prioritize patient-centered care, involving patients and their families in decision-making and treatment planning. This empowers patients, enhances satisfaction, and promotes adherence to care plans.

Challenges and Strategies for Effective Collaboration

While interdisciplinary collaboration offers significant benefits, it also presents challenges that must be addressed to ensure effective teamwork.

- Communication Barriers: Differences in terminology, communication styles, and professional hierarchies can hinder effective communication. Establishing clear communication protocols and fostering a culture of mutual respect can overcome these barriers.
- Role Clarity: Unclear roles and responsibilities can lead to confusion and duplication of efforts. Clearly defining the roles and contributions of each team member ensures that everyone understands their responsibilities and works cohesively.
- Interprofessional Education: Providing interprofessional education and training opportunities promotes understanding and respect among team members. Education initiatives should focus on collaborative skills, team dynamics, and the importance of interdisciplinary care.
- Leadership and Coordination: Effective leadership and coordination are essential for successful interdisciplinary collaboration. Designating a team leader or coordinator to facilitate communication, manage conflicts, and ensure that care plans are implemented smoothly can enhance team performance.
- Time Constraints: Busy schedules and competing priorities can limit opportunities for collaboration. Allocating dedicated time for team meetings, case discussions, and joint decision-making ensures that collaboration remains a priority.

Future Directions in Interdisciplinary Collaboration

The future of interdisciplinary collaboration in respiratory medicine holds promise for further enhancing patient care and advancing the field.

- Integrated Care Models: Developing and implementing integrated care models that promote interdisciplinary collaboration across healthcare settings will improve continuity of care and patient outcomes. These models should emphasize coordinated care, shared decision-making, and seamless transitions between providers.

- Technology and Collaboration: Leveraging technology, such as electronic health records (EHRs), telehealth, and collaborative platforms, will facilitate communication and information-sharing among interdisciplinary teams. These tools can enhance real-time collaboration and support patient-centered care.
- Research and Innovation: Collaborative research efforts involving interdisciplinary teams will drive innovation in respiratory medicine. By bringing together diverse expertise, researchers can address complex questions, develop novel interventions, and translate scientific discoveries into clinical practice.
- Patient and Family Engagement: Engaging patients and their families as active participants in the interdisciplinary care team will enhance patient satisfaction and outcomes. Providing education, support, and resources to patients and families empowers them to contribute to care planning and decision-making.

DISCUSSION QUESTIONS

- How does interdisciplinary collaboration contribute to innovation and improved patient care in respiratory medicine, and what are some examples of successful interdisciplinary initiatives that have positively impacted patient outcomes?
- What are the key barriers to effective interdisciplinary collaboration in respiratory medicine, and how can healthcare organizations foster a culture of collaboration, communication, and mutual respect among diverse healthcare professionals to overcome these barriers?

CONCLUSION

The field of respiratory medicine stands at the intersection of groundbreaking innovation and collaborative interdisciplinary efforts aimed at improving patient outcomes, advancing scientific knowledge, and addressing the complex challenges of respiratory health. Throughout this exploration of innovations in respiratory medicine, from diagnostic technologies to therapeutic interventions, environmental influences to future directions, several key themes have emerged.

First and foremost, technological advancements have revolutionized the diagnosis, treatment, and management of respiratory diseases, offering unprecedented opportunities for precision medicine, personalized care, and remote monitoring. From artificial intelligence-driven diagnostics to wearable devices and telemedicine platforms, these innovations empower healthcare providers to deliver more efficient, accurate, and patient-centered care, while also posing ethical considerations and challenges that require careful navigation and proactive solutions.

In navigating the complexities of respiratory medicine, collaboration, innovation, and equity must remain central tenets guiding our collective efforts to improve respiratory health outcomes and enhance the quality of life for individuals affected by respiratory diseases. By leveraging the power of innovation, embracing interdisciplinary collaboration, and advocating for health equity, we can chart a course toward a future where respiratory diseases are better understood, more effectively treated, and ultimately, prevented altogether. Together, we can breathe new life into respiratory medicine and pave the way for healthier futures for generations to come.

REFERENCES

Buist, A. S., McBurnie, M. A., Vollmer, W. M., Gillespie, S., Burney, P., Mannino, D. M., ... & Toelle, B. G. (2007). *International variation in the prevalence of COPD (the BOLD Study): a population-based prevalence study.*

Chung, K. F., Wenzel, S. E., Brozek, J. L., Bush, A., Castro, M., Sterk, P. J., ... & Adcock, I. M. (2014). *International ERS/ATS guidelines on definition, evaluation and treatment of severe asthma. European Respiratory Journal.*

GBD 2019 Diseases and Injuries Collaborators. (2020). *Global burden of 369 diseases and injuries in 204 countries and territories, 1990–2019: a systematic analysis for the Global Burden of Disease Study* 2019.

GINA Science Committee. (2021). *Global strategy for asthma management and prevention, 2021. Global Initiative for Asthma (GINA).*

Sessler, C. N., Gosnell, M. S., Grap, M. J., Brophy, G. M., O'Neal, P. V., Keane, K. A., ... & Molitoris, B. A. (2002). *The Richmond Agitation-Sedation Scale: validity and reliability in adult intensive care unit patients. American Journal of Respiratory and Critical Care Medicine.*

Vogelmeier, C. F., Criner, G. J., Martinez, F. J., Anzueto, A., Barnes, P. J., Bourbeau, J., ... & Han, M. K. (2017). *Global strategy for the diagnosis, management, and prevention of chronic obstructive lung disease 2017 report: GOLD executive summary. American Journal of Respiratory and Critical Care Medicine.*

www.ingramcontent.com/pod-product-compliance
Lightning Source LLC
Chambersburg PA
CBHW070441010526
44118CB00014B/2139